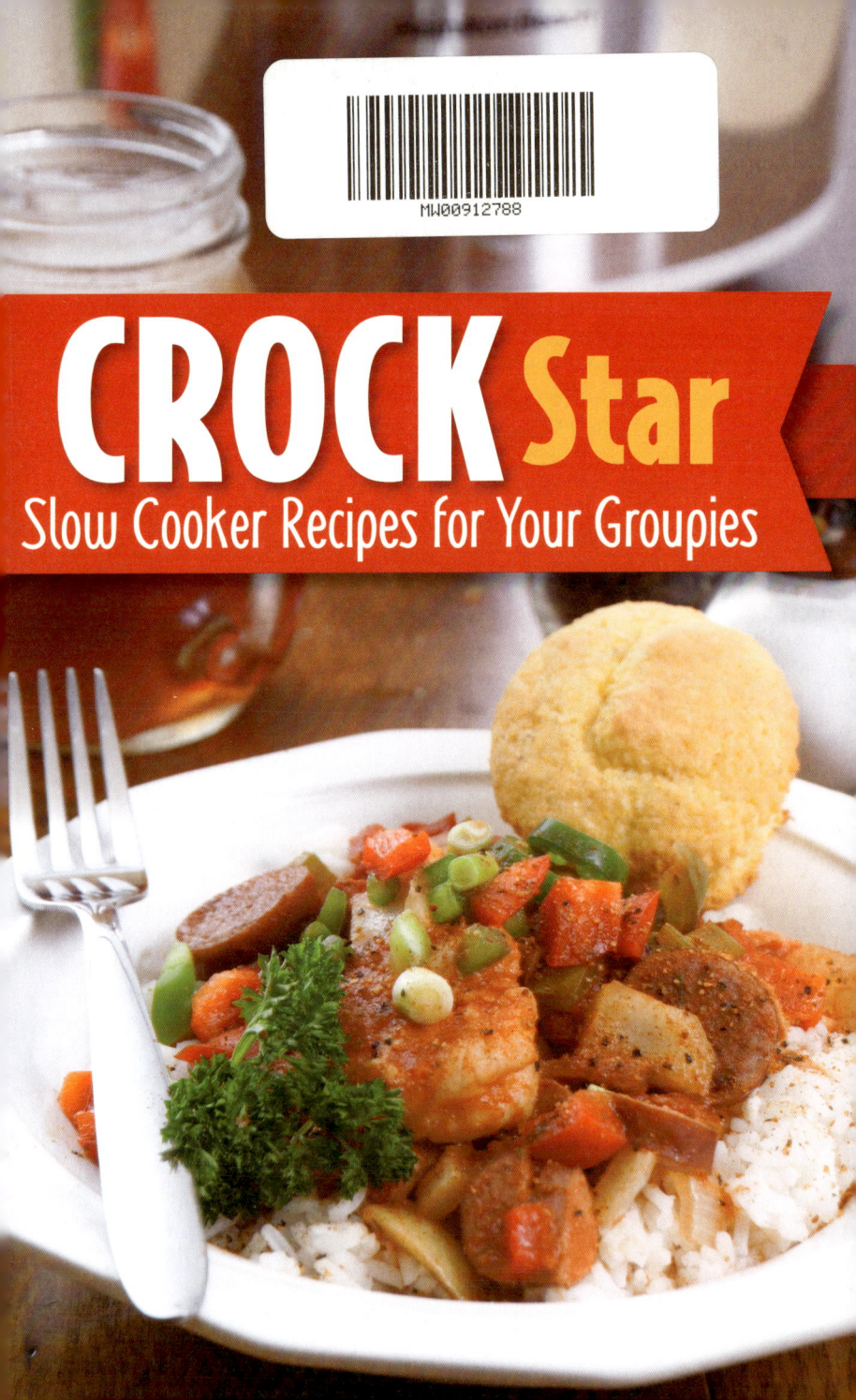

CROCK Star
Slow Cooker Recipes for Your Groupies

Copyright © 2013 CQ Products
Waverly, IA 50677
All rights reserved.
No part of this book may be reproduced or transmitted in any form or by any means, electronic or mechanical, including photocopying, recording or by any information storage and retrieval system, without permission in writing from the publisher.

Printed in the United States of America
by G&R Publishing Co.

Distributed By:

507 Industrial Street
Waverly, IA 50677

ISBN-13: 978-1-56383-480-6
ISBN-10: 1-56383-480-4
Item #7086

Follow these slow cooker tips to help you achieve crock star status:

★ Many recipes can be cooked equally well on high or low power. Generally, it takes about twice as long on low as it does on high. Feel free to experiment with different temperatures and times.

★ If your slow cooker is a different size than what's recommended in a recipe, adjust the cooking time – less time if using a larger cooker and more time if using a smaller one.

★ For best results, fill your slow cooker between ½ and ⅔ full, if possible.

★ Your slow cooker's insert could crack if exposed to sudden temperature changes. If the insert has been refrigerated, let it set at room temperature for 30 minutes before cooking. After cooking, let it cool for 30 minutes before refrigerating.

★ Thaw frozen meats and vegetables before placing in your slow cooker. Adding frozen food could cause the cooking temperature to drop below recommended safe temperatures.

★ Unless specified otherwise in a recipe, keep your slow cooker covered as much as possible while cooking, since removing the lid releases heat and may interfere with cooking time.

★ Some slow cookers have a "hot spot." If you notice this with yours, rotate the insert halfway through cooking time to ensure even cooking. This is especially important when making breads, desserts, and other dense foods.

★ As with any cooking, make sure food is thoroughly cooked before serving.

★ Typically, when making items like soups, it's best to add dairy products, such as sour cream or yogurt, toward the end of cooking time.

★ High altitude generally extends the cooking time one hour (on low) for every 4,000 feet.

serves 8 to 10

 low 5-6 hrs.

Saucy Meatballs

Ingredients

- 1 (28 oz.) can crushed tomatoes
- ½ C. beef broth
- 1 (6 oz.) can tomato paste
- 1 T. sugar
- 1 onion, chopped
- 1½ tsp. minced garlic
- Salt and red pepper flakes to taste
- 1 lb. each lean ground beef and ground pork
- ⅓ C. Italian bread crumbs
- 1 egg
- ¼ C. milk
- ¼ C. grated Parmesan cheese
- Cooked spaghetti

Directions

In a 4-quart slow cooker, stir together tomatoes with juice, beef broth, tomato paste, sugar, onion, garlic, salt, and red pepper flakes; set aside.

In a large bowl, mix ground beef, ground pork, bread crumbs, egg, milk, Parmesan, and more salt and red pepper flakes. Using a rounded tablespoonful, shape mixture into 30 balls; place in cooker and submerge in sauce.

Cover and cook on low for 5 to 6 hours or until meatballs are cooked through. Skim grease from sauce before serving with spaghetti.

Bun time...

Place meatballs and a little sauce on French rolls; top with shredded mozzarella.

Coffee Cake Surprise

- ¾ C. caramel topping
- ¼ C. plus 2 T. brown sugar
- ¾ tsp. ground cinnamon
- 6 T. plus 2¼ C. biscuit baking mix, divided
- 1 C. plus 2 T. sugar
- ¾ C. sour cream or vanilla yogurt
- 1 egg plus 1 egg yolk, lightly beaten
- 1½ tsp. vanilla extract

serves about 8

high 1¾–2¼ hrs.

Directions

Coat a 4-quart slow cooker with cooking spray and line with parchment paper. Pour caramel topping into an 8-ounce canning jar. Place lid and ring on jar, but do not tighten completely; set jar in the center of cooker. Coat jar and paper with cooking spray; set aside.

In a medium bowl, stir together brown sugar, cinnamon, and 6 tablespoons baking mix; set aside. In a large bowl, stir together remaining 2¼ cups baking mix, sugar, sour cream, egg, egg yolk, and vanilla until well blended. Spread half the batter around jar in cooker. Sprinkle with half the set-aside streusel mixture; repeat layers.

Place a double layer of paper towels over opening in cooker, making sure towels extend beyond the opening.* Cover and cook on high for 1¾ to 2¼ hours or until a toothpick inserted halfway between jar and side of cooker comes out clean. Uncover, remove insert from cooker, and let set for 10 minutes. Using a pot holder, carefully remove jar from insert by twisting and lifting. Remove coffee cake from insert by lifting parchment paper. Drizzle hot caramel over cake.

The paper towels help keep condensation from dripping off the lid onto the cake.

Hidden treasure…

The jar in the center not only gives your cake "Bundt appeal," but you can fill it with other toppings, like jam or honey.

serves about 10

low 4½ hrs. — 4 qt.

Green Beans Alfredo

Ingredients

- 2 (16 oz.) pkgs. frozen French-cut green beans, thawed
- 1 (15 oz.) jar Alfredo sauce
- 1 (8 oz.) can water chestnuts, drained and diced
- 1 (4 oz.) can sliced mushrooms, drained
- ¼ C. chopped roasted red peppers
- ⅓ C. grated Parmesan cheese
- ½ tsp. black pepper
- 1 (6 oz.) container French-fried onions, divided

Directions

Coat a 4-quart slow cooker with cooking spray; set aside.

In a large bowl, stir together green beans, Alfredo sauce, water chestnuts, mushrooms, red peppers, Parmesan, black pepper, and half the French-fried onions. Pour into prepared cooker.

Cover and cook on low for 4½ hours or until hot and bubbly. Top with remaining French-fried onions before serving.

Shown with...

Italian Beef (recipe on page 30). Get two slow cookers going and have a hot and hearty dinner waiting for you.

Chicken Enchilada Soup

- 1 lb. boneless, skinless chicken breasts
- 1 (15.2 oz.) can whole kernel corn, drained
- 1 (14.5 oz.) can diced tomatoes
- 1 (14.5 oz.) can chicken broth
- 1 (10 oz.) can enchilada sauce
- 1 (4 oz.) can diced green chiles
- 1 onion, chopped
- 1½ tsp. minced garlic
- 1½ tsp. chili powder
- Salt and black pepper to taste
- ¼ C. chopped fresh cilantro

fills 6 bowls

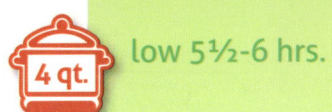

low 5½-6 hrs.

Directions

Coat a 4-quart slow cooker with cooking spray. Place chicken in cooker. Add corn, tomatoes with juice, chicken broth, enchilada sauce, green chiles, onion, garlic, chili powder, salt, black pepper, and cilantro; stir to blend.

Cover and cook on low for 5 hours or until chicken is cooked through. Then transfer chicken to a cutting board and shred meat. Return shredded meat to cooker; cover and cook 30 minutes to 1 hour more.

Set out...

bowls of chopped green onions, diced avocados, chopped fresh cilantro, and shredded Cheddar, letting everyone personalize their own soup.

serves 4

high 1¾-2¼ hrs.

Hawaiian Pizza

Ingredients

- 1 (13.8 oz.) tube refrigerated pizza crust
- ¾ C. pizza sauce
- Salt and black pepper to taste
- 1 to 2 C. shredded pizza cheese blend
- 1 (8 oz.) can pineapple tidbits, well drained
- 1 C. cubed ham
- ⅓ C. diced green bell pepper or jalapeño pepper

Directions

Line a 7-quart slow cooker with foil; coat foil with cooking spray. Unroll dough and place in prepared cooker, stretching to cover bottom and 1" up sides. Spread pizza sauce evenly over dough in bottom of cooker. Sprinkle with salt, black pepper, and pizza cheese. Arrange pineapple, ham, and bell pepper over cheese.

Cover and cook on high for 1¾ to 2¼ hours or until pizza begins to brown and pull away from foil. Then turn off cooker, uncover, and let set for 20 minutes. Remove pizza from cooker by lifting foil.

Flavor boost...

Cook sliced onion in 1 T. oil for 15 minutes or until caramelized. Add onion to pizza when cover is removed from cooker; let set as directed. Then, scatter baby spinach on top.

Blueberry French Toast

- 8 eggs
- ½ C. plain yogurt
- ⅓ C. sour cream
- 1 tsp. vanilla extract
- ½ tsp. ground cinnamon
- ¼ C. brown sugar
- 1 C. milk
- ⅓ C. pure maple syrup
- 1 (1 lb.) loaf French bread, cubed
- 1½ C. fresh blueberries
- 12 oz. cream cheese, cubed

serves about 8

 low 3-4 hrs.

Directions

Coat a 6-quart slow cooker with cooking spray; set aside.

In a large bowl, whisk together eggs, yogurt, sour cream, vanilla, cinnamon, and brown sugar until well beaten. Gradually whisk in milk and syrup until blended; set aside.

Place half the bread in prepared cooker, followed by half each of the berries, cream cheese, and egg mixture. Repeat layers.

Cover and refrigerate overnight. Remove from refrigerator 30 minutes before cooking. Then, cover and cook on low for 3 to 4 hours or until eggs are cooked through.

Sweet treat...

Just add a dusting of powdered sugar, your favorite syrup, and extra berries, if you'd like. What a yummy way to start your day!

Vegetable Lasagna

- 1 egg
- 1 (15 oz.) tub ricotta cheese
- 1 (6 oz.) pkg. baby spinach, coarsely chopped
- 3 Portobello mushroom caps (gills removed), thinly sliced
- 1 zucchini, thinly sliced
- 1 (28 oz.) can crushed tomatoes
- 2 (14.5 oz.) cans diced fire-roasted tomatoes
- 2 tsp. minced garlic
- 1½ tsp. each Italian seasoning and salt
- ½ tsp. black pepper
- 15 uncooked whole wheat lasagna noodles
- 3½ C. shredded mozzarella cheese, divided

serves about 8

low 4-5 hrs.

Directions

Coat a 6-quart slow cooker with cooking spray; set aside.

In a large bowl, stir together egg, ricotta, spinach, mushrooms, and zucchini; set aside. In a medium bowl, stir together all tomatoes with juice, garlic, Italian seasoning, salt, and black pepper. Spread 1½ cups tomato mixture in prepared cooker.

Arrange five noodles over tomato mixture in cooker, overlapping and breaking as needed to cover tomatoes. Spread half the ricotta mixture over the noodles and pat down firmly. Cover with 1½ cups tomato mixture and 1 cup mozzarella. Repeat layers. Arrange five noodles over the top, overlapping and breaking as needed; cover with remaining tomato mixture.

Cover and cook on low for 4 to 5 hours or until noodles are tender. Then turn off cooker and sprinkle remaining 1½ cups mozzarella over lasagna. Cover and let stand for 15 to 20 minutes or until cheese is melted.

Meat lovers...

Replace mushrooms with 1 lb. cooked and drained ground beef, adding onion if desired. Slow cook as directed.

serves 6

low 6 hrs.

7 qt.

Chicken Cordon Bleu

Ingredients

- 1 (10.7 oz.) can cream of chicken soup
- 2 tsp. minced garlic
- 1 tsp. seasoned salt
- ½ tsp. black pepper
- ½ C. milk
- 4 to 6 small boneless, skinless chicken breast halves*
- 6 slices deli ham
- 6 slices Swiss cheese
- 1 (6 oz.) pkg. chicken-flavored stuffing mix
- ¼ C. butter, melted

Directions

Coat a 7-quart slow cooker with cooking spray; set aside.

In a medium bowl, whisk together soup, garlic, seasoned salt, black pepper, and milk until well combined. Pour enough soup mixture into cooker to just cover the bottom. Arrange chicken in cooker and spread a little soup mixture over chicken. Cover each breast half with one slice each ham and Swiss. Pour remaining soup mixture over the top.

Cover and cook on low for 5 hours; then, sprinkle with stuffing mix and drizzle with butter. Cover and cook 1 hour more or until chicken is cooked through.

Number of chicken breasts depends on their size; it's best to keep them in a single layer, without stacking.

Roll it...

Flatten chicken breast halves to ½" thickness. Place one slice each ham and Swiss on each breast half and roll up, securing with toothpicks; arrange in cooker. Cook as directed.

Jambalaya

- 4 chicken thighs
- 1 lb. smoked sausage
- 1 each red and green bell pepper
- 1 jalapeño pepper, optional
- 2 to 3 canned chipotle peppers in adobo sauce
- 1 onion
- ½ C. sliced celery
- 1 (14.5) oz. can diced tomatoes
- 1 (6 oz.) can tomato paste
- 1¾ C. beef stock
- 2½ tsp. minced garlic
- 1 T. dried parsley
- 1½ tsp. each salt and cayenne pepper

Ingredients continued, next page

fills 12 bowls

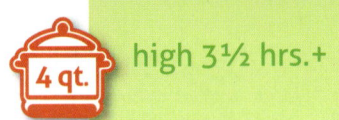

high 3½ hrs.+

Ingredients *continued*

½ lb. shrimp, peeled and deveined

1½ C. quick-cooking rice

Cajun seasoning to taste

Directions

Coat a 4-quart slow cooker with cooking spray; set aside.

Remove skin and bones from chicken thighs; cut into bite-size pieces and place in prepared cooker. Slice sausage and add to cooker.

Chop bell peppers, jalapeño pepper, chipotle peppers, and onion; place in a bowl. Stir in celery, tomatoes with juice, tomato paste, beef stock, garlic, parsley, salt, and cayenne pepper. Pour over meat in cooker.

Cover and cook on high for 3½ hours. Then carefully stir in shrimp and rice.* Cover and cook 15 to 20 minutes more or until shrimp turn pink and rice is tender. Stir in Cajun seasoning, if desired.

* Or cook rice separately and serve with Jambalaya.

Reuse it...

Stuff leftover jambalaya into hollowed-out green bell peppers and bake at 375° for 20 minutes or until heated through.

Jambalaya-Stuffed Peppers

serves 10 to 12

 low 7-8 hrs.

Loaded Potatoes

Ingredients

10 to 12 red potatoes, thinly sliced

Salt and black pepper to taste

1 tsp. garlic salt

½ lb. bacon strips, cooked and crumbled

1 onion, finely chopped

1 (8 oz.) pkg. shredded sharp Cheddar cheese

¼ C. butter, cut into small pieces

Directions

Line a 6-quart slow cooker with foil; coat foil with cooking spray. Arrange half the potatoes in cooker; sprinkle with salt and black pepper. Add half each of the garlic salt, bacon, onion, Cheddar, and butter. Repeat layers.

Cover and cook on low for 7 to 8 hours or until potatoes are tender.

Just baked...

Wrap russet potatoes in foil and arrange in a slow cooker. Cover and cook on low about 6 hours or until potatoes are fork-tender; unwrap and split. Add your favorite yummy toppings.

Baked Russets

Turkey Dinner

- 1 (12 oz.) pkg. stuffing cubes
- 2 T. butter, softened and cut into pieces
- 1 onion, chopped
- 1 C. sliced fresh mushrooms
- ½ C. dried sweetened cranberries
- 6 carrots, cut into pieces
- 1 (3 to 3½ lb.) boneless turkey breast*
- ¼ tsp. dried basil
- ½ tsp. each salt and black pepper

*If turkey is encased in netting, leave netting in place to cook.

serves 6 to 8

 low 8-9 hrs.

Directions

Coat a 6-quart slow cooker with cooking spray. Put stuffing cubes in cooker and drizzle ½ cup hot water over the top. Layer butter, onion, mushrooms, cranberries, and carrots over stuffing. Set turkey breast on top and sprinkle with basil, salt, and black pepper.

Cover and cook on low for 8 to 9 hours or until turkey is cooked through.

Transfer turkey to a cutting board and cover loosely with foil; set aside. Thoroughly stir stuffing mixture in cooker and let set for 5 minutes. Then slice turkey and serve with stuffing mixture.

Serve with...

Cran-Orange Bread (recipe on page 26) for a perfect flavor combo.

makes 1 loaf

high 2-3 hrs.

4 qt.

Cran-Orange Bread

Ingredients

3 C. flour

1⅓ C. sugar

1 T. baking powder

¼ tsp. baking soda

¼ tsp. salt

⅔ C. nonfat dry milk

1 egg, beaten

¼ C. canola oil

1 C. dried sweetened cranberries

1 T. orange zest

½ C. each chopped pecans and semi-sweet chocolate chips

Directions

Coat a 4-quart slow cooker heavily with cooking spray; set aside.

In a large mixing bowl, stir together flour, sugar, baking powder, baking soda, and salt. In a separate bowl, whisk together dry milk and 2 cups hot water until dissolved; add to flour mixture. Add egg and oil; beat on medium speed for 2 minutes. Fold in cranberries, orange zest, pecans, and chocolate chips. Spread evenly in prepared cooker.

Cover and cook on high for 2 to 3 hours, checking for doneness occasionally. Bread is done when the top feels firm. Uncover and let set in cooker for 10 minutes before turning out on a wire rack to cool completely.

Just add...

butter, cream cheese, and/or orange marmalade to make this sweet bread the star of your table.

Upside-Down Cake

Butter for greasing slow cooker

¼ C. butter, cut into small pieces

¾ C. brown sugar

3 T. dark rum or pineapple juice

1 (20 oz.) can pineapple slices, juice reserved

8 maraschino cherries

¾ C. cake flour

¾ tsp. baking powder

½ tsp. ground cinnamon

¼ tsp. each ground nutmeg and salt

⅔ C. sugar

¼ C. butter, softened

1 egg plus 1 egg yolk

2 T. half & half

serves 8

high 2-2½ hrs.

4 qt.

Directions

Grease a 4-quart slow cooker with butter; line with parchment paper and grease the paper. Turn cooker to high. Scatter butter pieces in cooker; sprinkle with brown sugar and drizzle with rum. Arrange pineapple slices over brown sugar, overlapping slightly and pressing gently; place a cherry in the center of each slice. Set aside.

In a small bowl, sift together cake flour, baking powder, cinnamon, nutmeg, and salt. In a medium mixing bowl, beat sugar and ¼ cup softened butter until light and fluffy. Mix in egg and egg yolk. Slowly add half & half, ¼ cup reserved pineapple juice, and flour mixture, beating until well blended and smooth. Pour evenly over pineapple in cooker.

Place a double layer of paper towels over opening in cooker, making sure towels extend beyond the opening.* Cover and cook on high for 2 to 2½ hours or until cake springs back when touched in the center. Then turn off cooker and let set for 20 minutes. Use the parchment paper to lift cake from cooker. Carefully invert cake onto a serving plate.

The paper towels help keep condensation from dripping off the lid onto the cake.

Good idea...

Using your slow cooker to make dessert is a no-brainer when it turns out this showy and delicious!

serves 12 to 15

6 qt. low 7-8 hrs.

Italian Beef

Ingredients

- 4½ to 5 lbs. beef roast, such as chuck
- 1 (12 oz.) jar beef gravy
- 1 to 2 C. Zesty Italian salad dressing
- 3 T. canola oil
- 1 onion, sliced
- 1 green bell pepper, sliced
- Salt and black pepper to taste
- 12 to 15 sandwich buns
- Shredded mozzarella cheese

Directions

Coat a 6-quart slow cooker with cooking spray. Place roast in cooker and pour gravy over the top.

Cover and cook on low for 7 to 8 hours. Then transfer roast to a cutting board and shred meat. Discard juices from cooker. Return shredded meat to cooker and add as much dressing as desired; stir to coat meat. Then cover, turn off cooker, and let set for 30 minutes.

Meanwhile, in a large skillet over medium-high heat, heat oil. Add onion, bell pepper, salt, and black pepper, cooking until crisp-tender. Serve meat and vegetables on buns; sprinkle each with a little mozzarella.

Shown with...

Green Beans Alfredo (recipe on page 8) for a little bit of Italian flair.

fills 8 bowls

low 8 hrs.+

Chicken Tortellini Soup

Ingredients

- 1 lb. boneless, skinless chicken breasts
- 1 C. each sliced carrots and celery
- 1 C. chopped onion
- 2 tsp. minced garlic
- 1½ tsp. each salt and dried basil
- ½ tsp. each dried oregano and cayenne pepper
- 1 (14.5 oz.) can chicken broth
- 2 C. frozen cheese tortellini, thawed
- 1 C. fresh baby spinach
- 1 (12 oz.) can evaporated milk

Directions

Cut chicken into bite-size pieces and place in a 6-quart slow cooker. Add carrots, celery, and onion; set aside.

In a large bowl, stir together garlic, salt, basil, oregano, cayenne pepper, chicken broth, and 3½ cups water. Pour over chicken and vegetables in slow cooker.

Cover and cook on low for 8 hours. Then stir in tortellini. Turn cooker to high, cover, and cook 30 minutes more or until tortellini is tender. Turn off cooker; stir in spinach and evaporated milk. Let set until spinach is wilted.

Shake on...

Coarse black pepper and Parmesan cheese are all that's needed to garnish this simple soup. Add cornbread (try the one shown on page 52) and a green salad for a complete meal.

serves 6

low 3-3½ hrs.

Bacon-Wrapped Corn

Ingredients

- 6 T. butter, softened
- 2 tsp. minced garlic
- ½ tsp. each salt and dried dill weed
- 1 tsp. coarse black pepper
- 12 mini ears frozen sweet corn, thawed*
- 12 bacon strips, partially cooked
- ½ C. chicken broth
- 1 red bell pepper, chopped

Directions

In a small bowl, stir together butter, garlic, salt, dill weed, and black pepper. Spread about 1½ teaspoons butter mixture over each chunk of corn; wrap each with a bacon strip, pressing edges to seal or securing with toothpicks. Place as many chunks as possible in a single layer in a 6-quart slow cooker; stack any remaining chunks on top. Add chicken broth and bell pepper.

Cover and cook on low for 3 to 3½ hours or until corn is tender.

Or cut fresh sweet corn into 2½" chunks. Adjust cooking time, if necessary.

Side note...

Partially cooked bacon is still easily wrapped around the corn chunks. If it is cooked to the crisp stage, wrapping will be very difficult. Bacon will finish cooking in the slow cooker.

Easy Minestrone

- 1 each onion, zucchini, and cabbage
- 2 potatoes
- ½ C. dry white beans
- 1 T. minced garlic
- 1 (14 oz.) can diced tomatoes
- ½ C. chopped carrot
- 2 T. Italian seasoning
- 2 tsp. each sugar and dried thyme
- Salt and black pepper to taste
- 2 tsp. red wine vinegar
- 6 to 6½ C. vegetable stock

fills 10 bowls

6 qt. low 9-10 hrs.

Directions

Chop onion, zucchini, cabbage, and potatoes; put into a 6-quart slow cooker. Stir in beans, garlic, tomatoes with juice, carrot, Italian seasoning, sugar, thyme, salt, and black pepper. Drizzle with vinegar and pour vegetable stock over all.

Cover and cook on low for 9 to 10 hours or until vegetables are tender.

Garnish with...
Parmesan cheese and chopped fresh parsley. Hot and satisfying!

fills 8 tortillas

low 3½ hrs.

Huevos Rancheros

Ingredients

1 T. butter

10 eggs, beaten

1 C. half & half

1 (8 oz.) pkg. shredded Mexican cheese blend

½ tsp. black pepper

½ tsp. minced garlic

¼ tsp. chili powder

1 (4 oz.) can diced green chiles

8 (6") corn tortillas

1 to 2 tsp. olive oil

Directions

Grease a 2-quart slow cooker with butter, leaving any remaining butter in cooker; set aside.

In a large bowl, whisk together eggs and half & half until well blended. Stir in Mexican cheese, black pepper, garlic, chili powder, and chiles. Pour into prepared cooker.

Cover and cook on low for 3½ hours. Then turn off cooker.

Fry tortillas, one at a time, in hot oil until lightly browned and bubbly; drain on paper towels and cover with foil to keep warm.

Serve eggs on tortillas.

Add on...

chopped tomato, jalapeño, or green bell pepper; refried or black beans; enchilada or hot sauce; lettuce or arugula... The options are endless.

Teriyaki Pork

- 1 (3 to 4 lb.) boneless pork roast*
- 1 C. brown sugar
- 1 onion, sliced and separated into rings
- ⅓ C. pineapple juice
- ⅓ C. soy sauce
- 1 tsp. minced garlic
- 1 tsp. ground ginger
- Salt and black pepper to taste
- 2 T. cornstarch

* If roast is encased in netting, leave netting in place to cook.

serves about 8

low 5-6 hrs.+

4 qt.

Directions

Coat a 4-quart slow cooker with cooking spray.

Coat roast with brown sugar and place in prepared cooker; add onion. Set aside.

In a small bowl, stir together pineapple juice, soy sauce, garlic, and ginger; pour over roast in cooker. Sprinkle with salt and black pepper.

Cover and cook on low for 5 to 6 hours or until roast is cooked to about 135°; transfer roast to a bowl. Strain solids from juices, returning juices to cooker and discarding solids; turn cooker to high. In a small bowl, stir together cornstarch and 3 tablespoons cold water until smooth. Gradually stir into juices in cooker. Return roast to cooker. Cover and cook on high for 45 minutes or until juices have thickened and roast is cooked through. Slice roast and serve with thickened gravy.

Delicious idea...

After cooking, shred meat and stir into thickened juices. Pile onto buns and top with pineapple and red onion slices.

serves about 8

4 qt. low 4¾ hrs.

Deluxe Brownies

Ingredients

- ½ C. butter
- 2 (4 oz.) pkgs. bittersweet chocolate, chopped
- 1 C. sugar
- 3 eggs, lightly beaten
- 1¼ C. flour
- ¼ C. unsweetened cocoa powder
- ¾ tsp. baking powder
- ½ tsp. sea salt
- ½ C. finely chopped walnuts
- 1 C. semi-sweet chocolate chips

Directions

Coat a 4-quart slow cooker with cooking spray; line cooker with parchment paper and coat paper with cooking spray. Set aside.

Melt butter and chocolate together; stir in sugar and eggs. Combine flour, cocoa powder, baking powder, and salt; stir into chocolate mixture. Add walnuts and chocolate chips, stirring until just moistened. Spread evenly in prepared cooker.

Cover and cook on low for 4 hours. Then uncover and cook 45 minutes more or until about 1" around the outer edges appears done. (Brownies will look undercooked in the center, but will be set up as they cool.) Remove insert from cooker, uncover, and set on a wire rack to cool completely. Remove brownies from cooker by lifting parchment paper.

Dust with...

a little powdered sugar. No frosting needed. Simple. Delicious. And cooked in a slow cooker. How cool is that?!

Creamy Loaded Corn

- 1½ C. half & half
- 1 C. chopped onion
- 48 oz. frozen whole kernel corn, thawed, divided
- ¼ C. butter, cubed
- 1 tsp. sugar
- ½ tsp. each salt and black pepper
- 1 T. canola oil
- 2 C. shredded Pepper Jack cheese, divided
- ¼ lb. bacon, cooked and crumbled

serves about 12

low 3-4 hrs.

4 qt.

Directions

Coat a 4-quart slow cooker with cooking spray; set aside.

In a blender, combine half & half, onion, and about 2½ cups corn. Cover and blend until nearly smooth. Pour into prepared cooker. Stir in remaining corn, butter, sugar, salt, black pepper, oil, ½ cup Pepper Jack, and bacon.

Cover and cook on low about 3 hours or until corn is hot. Then, sprinkle remaining 1½ cups Pepper Jack over corn mixture; stir. Cover and continue cooking 30 minutes more or until cheese is melted.

Enhance with...

crumbled bacon and a handful of chopped chives to give this corn a pop of color and an even bigger boost of flavor.

serves about 12

7 qt. high 3-4 hrs.

Buffalo Chicken Pasta

Ingredients

2 (10.7 oz.) cans cream of chicken soup

1 C. buffalo wing sauce

1 onion, finely chopped

2½ lbs. boneless, skinless chicken breasts

Salt, black pepper, and garlic powder to taste

1½ (16 oz.) pkgs. uncooked penne pasta

1 (16 oz.) tub sour cream

½ C. ranch salad dressing

1 C. shredded mozzarella cheese

Directions

Coat a 7-quart slow cooker with cooking spray. Pour both cans soup and wing sauce into cooker; add onion and set aside.

Cut chicken into bite-size pieces and season with salt, black pepper, and garlic powder; add to prepared cooker and stir to combine.

Cover and cook on high for 3 to 4 hours or until chicken is cooked through. Then turn off cooker.

Cook pasta according to package directions; drain and add to chicken mixture. Stir in sour cream, salad dressing, and mozzarella. Let set a few minutes before serving.

Buffalo Chicken Wraps

New twist...

Omit pasta. Cook chicken as directed, but don't add sour cream, salad dressing, or mozzarella. Instead, pile chicken mixture onto flour tortillas; add some sour cream, salad dressing, and mozzarella to each.

Honey-Apple Pork

- 3 T. olive oil
- ¼ tsp. each ground nutmeg and ground cloves
- ½ tsp. ground cinnamon, plus more for sprinkling
- ⅓ C. honey, plus more for drizzling
- 2½ to 3 lbs. pork loin
- 2 Red Delicious apples

serves about 10

low 7 hrs.

4 qt.

Directions

In a large zippered plastic bag, combine oil, nutmeg, cloves, ½ teaspoon cinnamon, and ⅓ cup honey. Seal bag and squeeze to mix ingredients. Cut long crosswise slits in pork loin and place in bag with honey mixture. Close bag and turn several times to coat pork. Refrigerate overnight.

Coat a 4-quart slow cooker with cooking spray. Thinly slice 1½ apples and arrange in cooker. Remove pork from bag and place in cooker. Slice remaining ½ apple and push slices into slits in pork. Drizzle with a little honey and sprinkle with a bit of cinnamon.

Cook on low for 7 hours or until pork is cooked through.

Add buns...

Slice the pork for sandwiches. Top with BBQ sauce, mayo, banana peppers, or even apple butter.

49

serves 10 to 15

high 3-4 hrs.+

4 qt.

Fruited Rice Pilaf

Ingredients

- 1 C. each uncooked wild rice and brown rice, rinsed
- 2 T. butter, melted
- 1 (32 oz.) carton chicken broth
- 1 C. diced sweet onion
- ½ tsp. black pepper
- Zest and juice from 1 orange
- 1 (5.5 oz.) pkg. dried sweetened cherries
- 1 C. chopped toasted pecans*

Directions

Coat a 4-quart slow cooker with cooking spray. In cooker, stir together wild rice, brown rice, and butter. Stir in chicken broth, onion, black pepper, and orange zest.

Cover and cook on high for 3 to 4 hours or until rice is tender. Add cherries and fluff with a fork. Then turn off cooker, cover, and let set for 15 minutes.

Stir pecans into rice and drizzle orange juice over the top.

To toast, place pecans in a single layer in a dry skillet over medium heat for approximately 6 minutes or until golden brown.

Rice re-created...

Mix 4 C. leftover pilaf, 1 egg, 1 T. grated Parmesan, and 2 C. bread crumbs; form patties and fry in hot oil until heated through. Eat plain or serve on a bun with provolone cheese.

Rice Patties

Cooker Cornbread

1¼ C. flour
¾ C. yellow cornmeal
¼ C. sugar
1 T. plus 1½ tsp. baking powder

1 tsp. salt
1 egg, lightly beaten
¾ C. heavy cream
⅓ C. butter, melted

serves 8

2 qt. high 2-3 hrs.

Directions

Heavily coat a 2-quart slow cooker with cooking spray; set aside.

In a medium bowl, combine flour, cornmeal, sugar, baking powder, and salt; stir lightly. Add egg, cream, butter, and ¼ cup water. Stir until just moistened. Spread evenly in prepared cooker.

Cover and cook on high for 2 to 3 hours, or until a toothpick inserted in center comes out nearly clean. Remove insert from cooker, uncover, and set on a wire rack to cool. Run a knife around the sides of the cooker to loosen cornbread. Carefully invert cooker and turn cornbread out onto a cutting board or wire rack.

Good eats...

Let bread cool slightly before cutting. Then serve with butter and jam or honey.

serves about 6

low 6½-7½ hrs.

2 qt.

Pumpkin Dessert

Ingredients

- 1 (15 oz.) can pumpkin
- 2 (5 oz.) cans evaporated milk
- 2 oz. spiced rum
- ¾ C. brown sugar
- ⅔ C. biscuit baking mix, divided
- 2 eggs, lightly beaten
- 2 tsp. pumpkin pie spice
- 2 T. butter, cut into pieces
- ¼ C. sugar

Directions

Coat a 2-quart slow cooker with cooking spray; set aside.

In a large bowl, stir together pumpkin, evaporated milk, rum, brown sugar, 3½ tablespoons baking mix, eggs, and pumpkin pie spice. Pour mixture into prepared slow cooker. Scatter butter on top; sprinkle with sugar and remaining baking mix.

Cover and cook on low for 6½ to 7½ hours or until mixture is thick and top is golden brown.

Just add...

a dollop of whipped topping and a sprinkle of nutmeg. Served warm or cold, this dessert is just the right ending to your holiday meal or a nice treat any time of year.

Home-Style Chili

- 2 lbs. very lean ground beef, such as 93%
- 1 C. sliced celery
- ½ C. each chopped red, green, and yellow bell pepper
- 1 onion, chopped
- 2 (15 oz.) cans kidney beans (drain 1 can)
- 2 (14.5 oz.) cans diced tomatoes
- 1 (6 oz.) can tomato paste
- 2 tsp. each salt and chili powder
- 2 tsp. minced garlic
- 1 (10.7 oz.) can tomato soup
- ½ to 1 C. spicy tomato juice

serves about 15

low 6-8 hrs.

6 qt.

Directions

Crumble ground beef into a 6-quart slow cooker. Add celery, bell peppers, onion, kidney beans with remaining juice, tomatoes with juice, tomato paste, salt, chili powder, garlic, soup, and tomato juice. Stir to blend.

Cover and cook on low for 6 to 8 hours or until hot and bubbly and ground beef is cooked through.

Grab it...

Serve chili in individual bags of corn chips, topped with shredded lettuce and cheese, sliced black olives, and sour cream (and anything else you can dream up).

Walking Chili

serves about 8

4 qt. high 2 hrs.

Fiesta Mac & Cheese

Ingredients

- ¼ C. butter, melted
- 1 tsp. sea salt
- ½ tsp. each garlic powder, dry mustard, and black pepper
- 1 (12 oz.) plus 1 (5 oz.) can evaporated milk
- 1 (10.7 oz.) can nacho cheese soup
- 3 C. uncooked rigatoni pasta
- 2½ C. shredded Mexican cheese blend, divided
- 1 C. milk
- 2 T. olive oil
- 1 C. panko bread crumbs
- Pinch of cayenne pepper

Directions

Coat a 4-quart slow cooker with cooking spray. In cooker, whisk together butter, salt, garlic powder, dry mustard, black pepper, both cans evaporated milk, and soup. Stir in pasta and 1 cup cheese, making sure pasta is submerged.

Cover and cook on high for 1½ hours. Stir in milk and remaining 1½ cups cheese; cover and cook 30 minutes more or until cheese is melted and pasta is tender.

In a small saucepan over medium-low heat, heat olive oil. Add bread crumbs and cayenne pepper; cook for a few minutes until lightly browned. Sprinkle over macaroni before serving.

Stir in...

cooked, chopped bacon. It adds extra crunch and who doesn't love bacon?!

serves about 12

low 7-8 hrs.

6 qt.

Sausage & Egg "Bake"

Ingredients

- 1 (9.6 oz.) pkg. fully cooked frozen sausage links, thawed
- 1 (1 lb. 14 oz.) pkg. frozen shredded hash browns, thawed
- 2 C. shredded mozzarella cheese
- ½ C. grated Parmesan cheese
- ¼ C. chopped sun dried tomatoes in oil, drained
- ¾ C. sliced green onions
- 12 eggs
- ½ C. milk
- 1 tsp. dry mustard
- Salt to taste

Directions

Slice sausage links. Coat a 6-quart slow cooker with cooking spray. Place half the hash browns in an even layer in cooker. Top with half each of the sausage slices, mozzarella, Parmesan, sun dried tomatoes, and green onions. Repeat layers; set aside.

In a medium bowl, whisk together eggs, milk, dry mustard, and salt until well blended. Pour evenly over layers in cooker.

Cover and cook on high for 3 hours or until eggs are cooked through.

Switch it...

by substituting 2 cups fully cooked chopped ham for the sausage and 2 cups shredded Cheddar for the mozzarella.

serves 8

high 2 hrs.

4 qt.

Double Berry Cobbler

Ingredients

1¼ C. flour, divided

2 T. plus 1 C. sugar, divided

1 tsp. baking powder

¼ tsp. ground cinnamon

1 egg, lightly beaten

¼ C. milk

2 T. canola oil

⅛ tsp. salt

2 C. each fresh raspberries and blueberries

Ice cream, optional

Directions

Coat a 4-quart slow cooker with cooking spray; set aside.

In a large bowl, stir together 1 cup flour, 2 tablespoons sugar, baking powder, and cinnamon. In a small bowl, whisk together egg, milk, and oil; add to flour mixture and stir until just moistened. Spread batter evenly in prepared cooker. In a large bowl, mix salt, remaining ¼ cup flour, and remaining 1 cup sugar. Add raspberries and blueberries; stir until well coated. Scatter evenly over batter in cooker.

Cover and cook on high for 2 hours or until cake portion is done. Serve with ice cream, if you'd like.

Fresh idea...

Try this recipe using pitted cherries or sliced peaches, nectarines, or apricots. Fruit never tasted so good!

Index

Breads & Breakfasts
Blueberry French Toast 14
Coffee Cake Surprise 6
Cooker Cornbread 52
Cran-Orange Bread 26
Huevos Rancheros 38
Sausage & Egg "Bake" 60

Side Dishes
Bacon-Wrapped Corn 34
Baked Russets 23
Creamy Loaded Corn 44
Fiesta Mac & Cheese 58
Fruited Rice Pilaf 50
Green Beans Alfredo 8
Loaded Potatoes 22

Main Dishes
Buffalo Chicken Pasta 46
Buffalo Chicken Wraps 47
Chicken Cordon Bleu 18
Chicken Enchilada Soup 10
Chicken Tortellini Soup 32
Easy Minestrone 36
Hawaiian Pizza 12
Home-Style Chili 56
Honey-Apple Pork 48
Italian Beef 30
Jambalaya 20
Jambalaya-Stuffed Peppers 21
Rice Patties 51
Saucy Meatballs 4
Teriyaki Pork 40
Turkey Dinner 24
Vegetable Lasagna 16
Walking Chili 57

Desserts
Deluxe Brownies 42
Double Berry Cobbler 62
Pumpkin Dessert 54
Upside-Down Cake 28